the 100 best
postersofthecentury

campaign

the 100 best
postersofthecentury

P

CAMPAIGN IN ASSOCIATION WITH PROFILE BOOKS

First published in 1999 by
Profile Books Ltd
58A Hatton Garden
London EC1N 8LX
www.profilebooks.co.uk

Campaign
174 Hammersmith Road
London W6 7HB
www.campaignlive.com

Picture credits
The Advertising Archives; Abbott Mead Vickers BBDO; Bartle Bogle Hegarty; Bates UK; BMP DDB; CDP; Ciba Geigy; DMB&B; Dr Chris Mullin; Estate of Abram Games; FCB; Hans Schleger & Associates; Heinz; History of Advertising Trust; Imperial War Museum; J. Walter Thompson; London Transport Museum; Lowe Howard-Spink; M&C Saatchi; McCann-Erickson; Modus Publicity; Ogilvy & Mather; Oxo; Paul Eastwood; Infoplan; Portland Outdoor Advertising; Publicis; Rainey Kelly Campbell Roalfe; RHM Foods; Saatchi & Saatchi; Salvation Army; Shell; TBWA; Van den Bergh Foods; Victoria & Albert Museum; WCRS; Wieden & Kennedy; Young & Rubicam.

Acknowledgements
The Editor, *Campaign* and Profile Books would like to thank the following people and organisations for their help in producing this book: Allen Thomas; Bernard Barnett; D&AD; David Bernstein; Dennis Sullivan; Elizabeth Brough; History of Advertising Trust; Naomi Games and the Estate of Abram Games; Trevor Beattie; Jenny Watts; Dr. Chris Mullin; Pat Schleger; Marion Henrion.

Edited by Tracey Taylor
Designed by Senate

Printed and bound by South Sea International Press, Hong Kong

A CIP catalogue record for this book is available from the British Library.

ISBN 1 86197 201 6 (softback)
ISBN 1 86197 224 5 (special edition hardback)

FOREWORD

How do you go about choosing the 100 best British posters of the century, given that hundreds of thousands were produced during that period? *Campaign* decided to bring together 12 specialists, drawn from the world of advertising, to form a selection panel. Most of its members have, at some time during their distinguished careers, produced advertising posters. Many of these posters have won awards. In addition, one or two of our luminaries have written books on the subject. With their combined experience and knowledge, an authoritative choice was guaranteed.

Next *Campaign* needed to source the raw material. This task was tackled by the book's editor, Tracey Taylor, who drew on the expertise of organisations such as the Victoria & Albert Museum, the History of Advertising Trust and D&AD to compile a long-list of posters.

Every jury member was also asked to do his own research before the panel met. There were obvious choices that appeared on everyone's list, which enabled the day's judging to get off to a good start. But then the real debate began in earnest.

Inevitably there were areas of disagreement. Opinion was divided when the controversial Benetton and Club 18-30 campaigns came up for discussion, for instance. Was the former gratuitous, the latter merely bad taste? Eventually the argument swung in favour of including both campaigns (see pages 91 and 100).

Every individual poster that was considered worthy was voted on and the long- list was pared down. As the panel worked its way through the century, it became apparent that the low points for advertising posters came at the beginning of the century and then during

the 1950s and 1960s. At the turn of the century the commercial poster was still in its infancy so masterpieces were few and far between, while the dearth of good work in the 1950s and 1960s can largely be attributed to the advent of commercial television.

By contrast, the 1970s and 1980s produced a glut of wonderful work. This era was dominated by Collett Dickenson Pearce, an advertising agency which championed the poster as a powerful medium to support television campaigns.

All the posters in this book warrant being included because of the originality, lateral thinking and skill of execution that went into creating them. And it is worth considering those people – clients, artists and agencies – who are responsible for their existence. Faced with something to sell, a brief and a blank sheet of paper, a creative mind wrestles to get an idea. But at the back of that mind there lies the knowledge that no matter how good the idea, it is always subject to the client's veto.

Many clients will insist you show a large picture of the product, with the logo reproduced bigger than it needs to be. They may want to include more words than is ideal, a telephone number or a web-site address. So, as well as a battle in their minds, agency creative directors have one on their hands too.

Posters need to be simple. Look at those for Victory V, Fiat 132, the Tate Gallery by Tube and VW Polo (pages 67, 68, 84, and 107) and you will see the poster at its very best: brief, lateral and bold.

We should applaud all the creative minds behind these 100 posters and the clients that approved them This book is a great tribute to them.

Ron Brown, Chairman of Selection Panel

THE PANEL: The panel of leading creative directors and poster specialists that selected the posters in this book. Sitting, left to right: Robert Campbell, co-creative director, Rainey Kelly Campbell Roalfe/Y&R; Tracey Taylor, editor of this book, editor and writer specialising in media and advertising; Alan Waldie, art director, former deputy chairman, Lowe Howard-Spink and art director, Collett Dickenson Pearce; Ron Brown (chairman of the selection panel), executive head of art, Abbott Mead Vickers BBDO; Larry Barker, creative director, BMP DDB; Tony Cox, creative director, Abbott Mead Vickers BBDO; Patrick Collister, creative director, Ogilvy & Mather. Standing, left to right: Dennis Sullivan, chairman and CEO, Portland Outdoor Advertising; Stefano Hatfield, editor *Campaign*; David Bernstein, founder of The Creative Business and author of *Advertising Outdoors*; Alfredo Marcantonio, executive creative director, D'Arcy Europe; Allen Thomas, worldwide creative director, J. Walter Thompson; Trevor Beattie, creative director, TBWA; Ron Zeghibe, chief executive officer, Maiden Outdoor.

INTRODUCTION

'Painting is an end in itself. The poster is only a means to an end, a means of communication between the dealer and the public, something like a telegraph. The poster designer plays the part of a telegraph official: he does not initiate news; he merely dispenses it. No-one asks him for his opinion, he is only required to bring about a clear, good and exact connection.'
Cassandre (Jean-Marie Moreau), 1933.

'I have made this letter longer than usual, only because I have not had the time make it shorter.' Blaise Pascal, 1657.

This is a book about the best commercial posters of the 20th century, those which we recognise immediately today as advertising. It limits itself to Britain in the hope of tracing the development of the advertising medium in this country more exactly. It does not include posters for art exhibitions, plays and films, which are often commissioned as works of art in their own right, because these operate under entirely different rules.

However, in order to tell this story we must begin in France in the 19th century with a man who fought to be recognised as an artist, and who first came to prominence designing artistic posters for one-off theatrical events.

The origins of the commercial poster are usually traced back to the work of French artist Jules Cheret. From 1866 onwards Cheret took advantage of new developments in colour lithography to adapt the techniques of the lithographic book illustrator to a wider canvas.

He took the popular folk art that was being used at the time for the covers of circus programmes and enlarged it, to what would now be known as the 16-sheet poster size. His appeal to the consumer's senses through the use of colour and design represented the poster medium's first move away from merely describing or illustrating the product being sold.

It was the birth of the commercial poster as we know it today. At the time, Cheret was embroiled in a major debate over the status of poster design in France, a country where the academies had elevated the status of fine art over applied art. The 'is it art, or just advertising?' debate continues to this day. Cheret and his contemporaries, Henri de Toulouse-Lautrec and Pierre Bonnard, were successful in crossing the line

between the two. Cheret's work was so admired that clients – ranging from department stores and bookshops to pharmaceutical and cosmetics manufacturers – would ask him to create new designs rather than repeat his posters. Some art dealers began trading in posters.

Most poster advertisements in Britain at the turn of the century were, by contrast, unimaginative. More often than not they featured only the manufacturer's name in a huge typeface, and perhaps a picture of the product. There were precious few advertising copylines or attempts to transform the product into a brand.

The notable exceptions to this blandness came from the rival soap manufacturers, Lord Leverhulme of Sunlight and T.J. Barratt of Pears Soap. The most famous of the pre-20th century British advertising images, 'Bubbles', painted by Sir John Millais, had been bought by Barratt in 1886. The chromo-lithographic print was praised for its reproductive quality, but many commentators believed the use of the painting to sell soap degraded art.

The explosion of the poster medium in the second half of the 19th century was a major contributor to the birth of advertising agencies as we know them today. The repeal of heavy newspaper taxes in the 1850s, the arrival of the steam train and the emergence of differentiated packaging and branding led to a boom in the volume of advertisements.

Where previously advertisers had created their own advertising in-house, and agencies placed the press ads, now they turned to early agencies such as Mather & Crowther and S.H. Benson to design press ads and 'manage' poster campaigns.

S.H. Benson was established to handle the Bovril account, and an early poster in its advertising campaign, 'Alas! My poor brother', with which we begin our chronological selection, is an excellent example of the sparse British style pioneered by the likes of Dudley Hardy and John Hassall. These artists, in contrast to their French peers, were primarily cartoonists.

The enduring impact of the British style today is due in no small part to its political incorrectness. Tastes change. What one generation finds shocking, another finds harmless – risible even. And, as the Bovril poster suggests, it is too simplistic to assume that we have become ever more liberal.

Early patrons of the commercial poster medium, such as Leverhulme and Barratt, were notable for using the poster as just one part of their marketing armoury. They believed in what has become the holy grail of the marketing services industry today: integrated campaigns. They, of course, didn't know they were taking a holistic, mixed-media approach; they were just using their common sense to sell more soap.

Another hugely influential patron was Frank Pick, the man who was responsible for publicity for London Transport from 1908 until 1940. Pick can be regarded as an early media planner. He recognised the need to break through the chaos that the largely unregulated development of the poster medium had allowed. Pick made a clear distinction between London Transport's advertisements and its public service information posters which were about station names and train times. He planned where and when the different types of posters would appear using a grid system, devised different sizes depending on the message, and greatly reduced clutter.

Pick became patron to and, in many cases, commissioned personally an extraordinary number of talented artists. Tom Eckersley, Austin Cooper, Fougasse, John Hassall, Edward McKnight Kauffer, Tom Purvis, Man Ray, Graham Sutherland, Fred Taylor and Rex Whistler were just some of the influential names whose skills he sought out.

Pick's philosophy was also significant. He was an early pioneer of 'soft sell' advertising. London Transport's posters rarely showed the means of transportation, but focused instead on the destination. Although in the early years there was a need to drive traffic through the relatively under-used system, once the rush hour had become a part of London life the main subject of the advertising was leisure.

Londoners were induced either to escape the bustle of the city, or to take advantage of its amenities. Either way, London Transport was sold to passengers as being the lifeblood of the city. Pick believed that one purpose of his advertising was 'the establishment of goodwill and good understanding between the passengers and the companies'.

Such early flowerings of what we might today refer to as corporate advertising were soon halted by the outbreak of the First World War. Although the most famous poster of the war years was unarguably Alfred Leete's 'Britons (Lord Kitchener) wants you' (later adapted by James Montgomery Flagg as 'I want you for U.S. Army'), it was another poster that helped to make the war years a seminal period in the development of British advertising.

Savile Lumley's 'Daddy, what did YOU do in the Great War?' was typical of its time in that it took an everyday sentimental image and, via a series of visual hints and a plaintive strapline, turned it into a powerful piece of emotional blackmail.

It is not so much the artistic merit of the poster that makes it so significant, rather the moral debate it inspired. Not during the war, of course, when it would have been deemed unpatriotic to have quibbled, but afterwards, when the senseless slaughter in the trenches became the subject of much recrimination.

The British government stood accused by its critics of using propaganda to mislead the public about the horrors of the war. Adolf Hitler didn't help matters much when he paid tribute to Britain's 'brilliant' and 'ruthless' First World War propaganda in *Mein Kampf*.

Although no-one denied the effectiveness of the propaganda campaign – which created a caricature of the ruthless Hun and cajoled men into enlisting – it prompted, almost for the first time, a public debate about the morality of advertising. It began to be seen as not just grubby, but tantamount to a black art.

This meant that the government had to be very careful about its post-war advertising. It could not afford to be seen to be deceiving the public. Its solution was to rise above the obvious hard sell and commission advertising of an artistic quality that was a cut above the rest. For example, the Empire Marketing Board's campaign to persuade the public to buy produce from Britain's dominions is as noticeable for its low-key approach as for its innovative graphic design.

Although the inter-war years saw the birth of some of Britain's most notable and long-running advertising campaigns – such as the fruits of John Gilroy's association with Guinness, the first flowerings of Shell's seminal campaigns under its advertising manager Jack Beddington, and the golden years of London Transport advertising – the Second World War was a catalyst for a magnificent array of styles and individual posters.

The re-established Ministry of Information employed some 60 artists, designers, typographers and printers. Mindful of the furore the Great War's campaigns had caused, and not needing a recruitment drive because conscription was already in place, the government's campaigning began gingerly during what has become known a the phoney war period of 1939-40.

The great posters, so etched in the memories of those who lived through that period came later. They were not overt appeals to nationalism or attempts to present Winston Churchill or Britain's other leaders as heroic figures in the Nazi or Soviet manner, but rational invitations to 'do your own bit'. The government was mindful this time around to ensure that this was everyone's war.

Perhaps the unique nostalgia provoked by the intensity of war has made some of the posters appear of more artistic merit than they are. But memorable slogans such as 'Dig for victory', 'Careless talk costs lives' and 'They also serve' remain with us today. And the work of artists such as Abram Games and Hans Schleger are still powerful and modern.

Radio and cinema became significant tools of government propaganda during the war. The family huddled around the wireless listening to Churchill's defiant exhortations to still greater courage and fortitude were the major media moments of the conflict. It was a foretaste of a period of relative decline for the outdoor medium after the war.

One by one successive illustrative art movements are represented in British posters of the first half of the century: art nouveau, art deco, cubism, modernism, expressionism, Dada, surrealism, Soviet art, constructivism. However, we must not make the mistake of believing it was the norm to commission artists to employ their talents in such a way.

This book and other collections like it display the best work. But the great mass of dreary poster advertising that appeared all over the country in the earlier part of the century, was to become the source of much controversy. The outcry led to the Council for the Protection of Rural England lobbying successfully for planning legislation which prevented a surfeit of the type of roadside hoardings so common in the United States and continental Europe.

Most commercial posters were anything but loved by the general public. Many sites had been commandeered by the government during the war and, as rationing and paper shortages meant that the commercial poster did not reappear until the end of the 1940s, after such a hiatus the medium was slow to reassert its potential.

The advent of commercial television in 1956 changed posters irrevocably. Now most advertisements were created within advertising agencies by a copywriter and art director team. The illustrator had become a graphic designer. Television became the lead medium, with posters reduced to playing a supporting role.

Photography began to usurp illustration as the medium's primary craft skill. Indeed, in many cases enlarged photographs and stills from the television campaign sufficed, allied to the newly dominant strapline. Although a couple of the better examples feature in this book, and great poster artists such as Games and Eckersley remained in demand, it was not a memorable period for the medium.

The thrill of the new lured talent into arenas other than television. The psychedelic movement of the 1960s, for example, is conspicuous by its absence from this book. The great examples of applied psychedelic art are to be found on record album covers and bill-posters advertising concerts and movies.

During the 1950s and 1960s a 'new advertising' began to emerge in the United States under the twin influences of Bill Bernbach (the co-founder of Doyle Dane Bernbach) and David Ogilvy (founder of Ogilvy & Mather). Bernbach pioneered the use of creative teams and reacted against the dominance of market research and demographics. He used ironic humour (most famously in the Volkswagen Beetle's 'Think small' advertisement). He raised the standing of the creative people within his agency at the expense of the account managers.

Ogilvy shared Bernbach's love of simplicity, but was an early pioneer of the use of market research tools. He detested what he regarded as 'frippery' in advertising, and had no time for 'artistic' ads (meaning illustration), preferring the realism of photography.

The two men's belief in simplification manifested itself in ads featuring black and white photography, a short headline, and some concise, explanatory body copy, usually in the bottom half of the page. Both Ogilvy and Bernbach achieved early success with press ads not posters.

Although both men were hugely influential, it took a campaign that was distinctly not of either school to resurrect the status of poster advertising in Britain: Collett Dickenson Pearce's Benson & Hedges advertisements of 1977. CDP was the agency leading Britain's own advertising revolution. It had used top fashion photographers to establish its creative reputation in the 1960s, and had assembled an extraordinary pool of talent in a creative department that produced ads for Hamlet, Heineken, Hovis and many more of the best campaigns in British television advertising history.

By 1977, it had become extremely difficult to advertise cigarettes. A full television ban was in effect and regulations prevented manufacturers associating the product with sexual or social success. Images of celebrities and young people were also banned, and each advertisement had to carry a government health warning.

Faced with such obstacles, Gallaher gave the agency an entirely open brief. Using the artist René Magritte as his inspiration, the art director, Alan Waldie, turned to some of the leading photographers of the time to create a surreal, intriguing campaign, which over time did away with the image of the cigarette packet or any copy at all. It was a campaign that acknowledged consumer's increased level of advertising literacy in the late 1970s. An enigmatic and even more surreal cinema commercial proved equally influential: audiences enjoyed solving the puzzle.

The Benson & Hedges campaign was a huge success. Not only did it increase sales of the brand, but also the creative innovation of the campaign (and the awards with which it was garlanded) attracted advertising creatives, particularly art directors, back to the medium.

But it was another, entirely different poster of the late 1970s that had the greater effect on the general public, and, arguably, the industry: the Conservative Party's 'Labour isn't working' ad, the most powerful British political poster of all time (see page 66). Although the poster appeared in 1978, the year before the election, it capitalised on the fear of mass unemployment prevalent at the time. The bold headline and the depiction of a queue of people outside an unemployment office were a combination that became seared in the public consciousness during the subsequent 'winter of discontent'. This was a period when Britain was beset by public-sector strikes, giving additional meaning to the idea that the country under Labour was not working.

Nevertheless, it is debatable whether the poster would have made quite as much impact if the Labour Prime Minister, James Callaghan, had not prolonged its life by publicly condemning it. Although it was by no means the reason why Margaret Thatcher defeated Callaghan, the poster certainly set the tone for the content of the campaign, forcing Callaghan into a defensive position from which he was unable to recover.

'Labour isn't working' not only made Maurice and Charles Saatchi household names, it focused attention back on the power of the poster. And, as the 1980s progressed, the medium slowly regained lost ground, as successive elections were fought out ever more aggressively.

The success of political campaigns demonstrated that advertisers did not have to spend a fortune on buying poster sites in order to get noticed. This proved particularly attractive as the boom years of the 1980s led to huge increases in the cost of television advertising airtime.

Many potential smaller advertisers were priced out of the medium and, with the poster contractors beginning the process of improving the quality and technology of their stock that continues today, clever advertisers such as *The Economist* and Nike took full advantage.

During the 1990s campaigns for Benetton, Wonderbra, French Connection, Pretty Polly and both the Conservative and Labour parties have all raised the profile of the medium. But not everyone in the advertising industry is entirely happy about it. Debates about the morality of the Benetton and French Connection campaigns, for example, echo those of earlier decades. The explosion of media on the back of the twin enablers of deregulation and technology has diminished the mass-market status of television and press advertising. The poster medium is, arguably, the only genuine mass medium left. Which brings with it certain responsibilities.

The poster industry's other problem is that some of the more high-profile recent campaigns – particularly those associated with the TBWA creative director Trevor Beattie – prove an agency does not have to spend an enormous sum of money on buying poster sites.

If you set out to ally the advertising to a PR campaign built on elements within the advertising, compliant journalists will provide your client with acres of free editorial space. Beattie's technique owes much to 'Labour isn't working' and the Saatchi brothers' knack of using controversy to their advantage.

Inevitably, these controversial campaigns have inspired many less clever imitators. Unscrupulous advertisers have abused the Advertising Standards Authority's role in policing printed advertisements by deliberately creating ads they hope will be banned. They then capitalise on the ensuing publicity.

The best posters of the 1990s bear testament to the fact that to use posters to their greatest effect, 'less is more'. There are an extraordinary number of posters today where that message is forgotten: too many elements compete for space; there is too much text; or the logo is so tiny and tucked away in the corner as to be illegible. It is advertisers' money poured down the drain.

The end of the century finds the medium in good shape, with ambient media, and other new forms of outdoor advertising providing genuinely exciting creative opportunities. The consolidation of ownership among the medium's contractors has enabled huge investments to be made in infrastructure and new formats. As the Internet and other interactive media focus increasingly on personalised marketing, the outdoor medium takes on an ever more potent role as the last true mass medium.

Although 'outdoor' accounts for just over 5% of total British advertising spend – a figure which should be improved upon – the applied imagination evident in the best of today's poster campaigns has produced a new golden age of creativity which easily rivals the heyday of 'artistic posters'.

Stefano Hatfield, Editor of *Campaign*

THE TOP TEN

Choosing the ten best posters of the century raises difficult questions. What constitutes a classic poster and did the same criteria apply in 1910 as they did in 1990? Can one compare the propaganda campaigns of the two world wars with advertisements for soap powder, beer or even bras?

Is it possible to select from such a wealth of great work just 10 posters that are each masterpieces in their own right and also represent the best of the best across 100 years?

The selection panel for this book was methodological in its approach to the task. First each panel member compiled his personal top ten list. These were amalgamated to produce an overall ranking. Then the panel voted for the best poster in each of the ten decades that make up the century. This list was put next to the first and discussed by the panel until agreement was reached on a final league.

The top ten includes a political campaign – 'Labour isn't working' which was voted the best single poster of the century – war posters, as well as a car stuck on a billboard and a newborn baby advertising sweaters. A controversial selection certainly, and no doubt one that will generate lively debate.

1

3

2

4

1   Conservative Party, Labour isn't working; 1978; p66
2   Parliamentary Recruiting Committee, Lord Kitchener wants you; 1914; p19
3   Gallaher/Benson & Hedges, Pyramids; 1977, p65
4   Arthur Guinness Sons & Company, Guinness for strength; 1934; p32
5   *The Economist*, Management trainee; 1989; p88
6   Health Education Council, Pregnant man; 1969; p58
7   Ciba Geigy, It also sticks handles to teapots; 1982; p75
8   Ministry of Information, Careless talk costs lives; 1940; p37
9   Benetton, Newborn baby; 1991; p91
10 Playtex, Hello boys; 1994; p99

"I never read The Economist."

Management trainee. Aged 42.

5

Would you be more careful if it was you that got pregnant?

Anyone married or single can get advice on contraception from the Family Planning Association. Margaret Pyke House, 27-35 Mortimer Street, London W1 N 8BQ. Tel. 01-636 9135.
The Health Education Council

6

It also sticks handles to teapots. ARALDITE

7

"Of course there's no harm in your knowing!"

CARELESS TALK COSTS LIVES

8

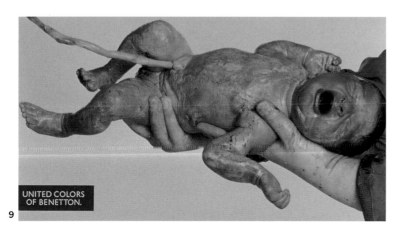

UNITED COLORS OF BENETTON.

9

10

HELLO BOYS.

THE ONE AND ONLY wonderbra

THE ORIGINAL PUSH-UP PLUNGE BRA. AVAILABLE IN SIZES 32-38 ABC.

THE 100 POSTERS OF THE CENTURY

A CHRONOLOGICAL CONTENTS LIST

Year: 1905
Title: Alas my poor brother
Client: Bovril
Original design (1896): W.H. Caffyn

It is questionable whether such an overt reference to a meat product's provenance would be used today in an advertisement. However the humour in this poster is as fresh now as it was nearly 100 years ago

Year: 1905
Title: Votes for women
Client: Women's Social and Political Union
Artist: H.M. Mallas

As with many of the best advertising slogans, this one came about by accident. Suffragettes Emmeline and Christabel Pankhurst originally produced a poster with the words 'Will you give votes for women?' which was to be displayed at a public meeting. The banner was replaced with a smaller placard and three words were cut out to fit the space. It took 13 more years for the campaigners' demand to be realised

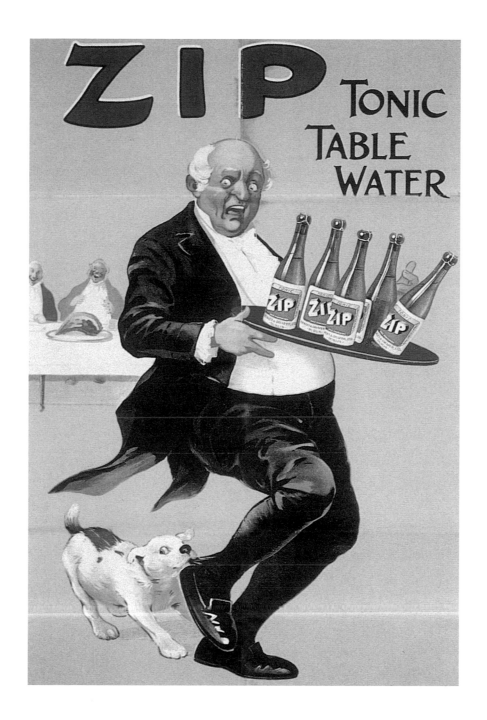

Year: 1907
Title: Waiter and dog
Client: Zip
Artist: Unknown

Its use of vivid colour and its
cheeky sense of humour helped
to make this poster stand out
from the crowd in the early
1900s. It marked an early use
of a narrative style in poster
advertising

Year: 1908
Title: Skegness is so bracing
Client: Great Northern Railway; reissued by the LNER
Artist: John Hassall

The great poster artist John Hassall believed the essentials of a successful poster were 'simplicity and a huge splash of colour' which would 'hit the passer-by right in the eyeball...'. This comic Hassall character has been indelibly linked to the town of Skegness since the illustration was first issued in 1908

Year: 1909
Title: Smoke Ogden's Midnight Flake
Client: Ogden's
Artist: Unknown

In this early narrative poster for the Ogden's pipe tobacco brand, the passer-by is drawn in by the image which hints at a wider story

Before Oxo became a cube it was a liquid beef extract called Fluid Oxo, for which this is an early advertisement. The origins of the Oxo name are not known, but the three letters have been a gift for artists and advertising agencies down the century, including here where they are incorporated into the narrative of the poster

"WORKLESS"

PUBLISHED BY THE LABOUR PARTY, 28 VICTORIA STREET, LONDON, S.W. & PRINTED BY DAVID ALLEN & SONS LD. HARROW. ETC.

Year: 1910
Title: Workless
Client: Labour Party
Artist: Gerald Spencer Pryse

A powerful image to depict the hopelessness of unemployment was here used to great effect by the Labour Party during a general election in 1910. It was an idea that was to be echoed some seven decades later when the Conservative Party took up the theme in its advertising – and toppled the then Labour government in the process (see page 66)

Year: 1910
Title: To the rescue
Client: Martell's Brandy
Artist: Unknown

The positive image of a St. Bernard mountain rescue dog became associated with the Martell brand after this poster advertisement appeared in 1910

Year: 1912
Title: Blackpool
Client: Blackpool
Artist: John Hassall

Poster artist John Hassall was known for his popular sense of humour. Here, however, he eschewed comedy and produced a quietly compelling image with a strong sense of unity to entice people to the seaside resort of Blackpool

Proclaimed on all hands

Matchless for the Complexion

10: 1912
Title: Proclaimed on all hands
Client: Pears Soap
Artist: Unknown

The Pears soap company took advertising very seriously. Its campaigns ran for more than 70 years, beginning in the mid-1800s. In this, surreal poster the brand is given a deity-like status. The accompanying poster, 'Bubbles', painted by Sir John Millais, first appeared before the turn of the century but its popularity ensured it continued to be seen well into the 20th century

Year: 1914
Title: Lord Kitchener wants you
Client: Parliamentary Recruiting Committee
Agency: Caxton Advertising
Artist: After Alfred Leete
Copywriter: Eric Field

This depiction of Lord Kitchener commanding young men to sign up has become one the century's great iconic images. The now famous line, 'Your country needs you', which appears in the accompanying poster above, was used as part of the same campaign

Daddy, what did **YOU** do in the Great War?

Year: 1915
Title: Daddy what did you do in the Great War?
Client: Parliamentary Recruiting Committee
Artist: Savile Lumley

The emotion conveyed in this poster, commissioned to encourage men to enlist, is encapsulated in the expression on the face of the father as he ponders how to answer his daughter's question. The whole image, down to the young boy playing with his toy soldiers, tells a compelling story

Year: 1918
Title: Put strength in the final blow
Client: National War Savings Committee
Artist: Frank Brangwyn

The full horror of the reality of war was powerfully depicted in this poster by the Belgian artist Frank Brangwyn, which appeared only a few weeks before the end of the hostilities. The National War Savings Committee was reportedly shocked when it first saw the image but agreed that 'nothing could be too drastic to fight the Germans with'

Year: 1919
Title: Soaring to success
Client: *Daily Herald*
Artist: Edward McKnight Kauffer

The strong graphic image created by Edward McKnight Kauffer for this poster was used by the *Daily Herald* to suggest both the heights of success reached by the newspaper and the concept of the 'early bird' getting the best news

Year: 1920
Title: Prevents that sinking feeling
Client: Bovril
Agency: S.H. Benson
Artist: H.H. Harris

Bovril's advertising agency,
S.H. Benson, came up with one of
the first copylines to enter the
collective memory in this
charming, funny poster where the
brand reigns supreme

THE MIGHTY ATOM

ONE CUBE MAKES A NOURISHING BEEF DRINK

DISSOLVE IN A CUP OF HOT WATER

OXO CUBE

Concentrated Energy of Beef

Year: 1922
Title: The mighty atom
Client: Oxo
Artist: Unknown

Oxo here exploited the scale of the medium to convey the strength and power both of its product and its brand. The herd of cattle shown at the foot of the poster appear strangely unperturbed by the appearance of a gigantic, even atomic, Oxo cube in their midst

Year: 1925
Title: Ah! Bisto
Client: Cerebos/Bisto
Artist: Will Owen

The Bisto Kids, invented by artist Will Owen in 1919, have secured a place in the hearts and minds of several generations. Depicted as cheeky street urchins, they immortalised the 'Ah! Bisto' line in a series of drawings showing them savouring the aroma of gravy made with Bisto

Year: 1925
Title: East Coast by LNER
Client: LNER
Artist: Tom Purvis

Tom Purvis was one of five commercial artists contracted to work exclusively for the London North East Railways (LNER) in the late 1920s and early 1930s. Purvis's style, using flat colour and the minimum of detail, remains as appreciated today as it was then

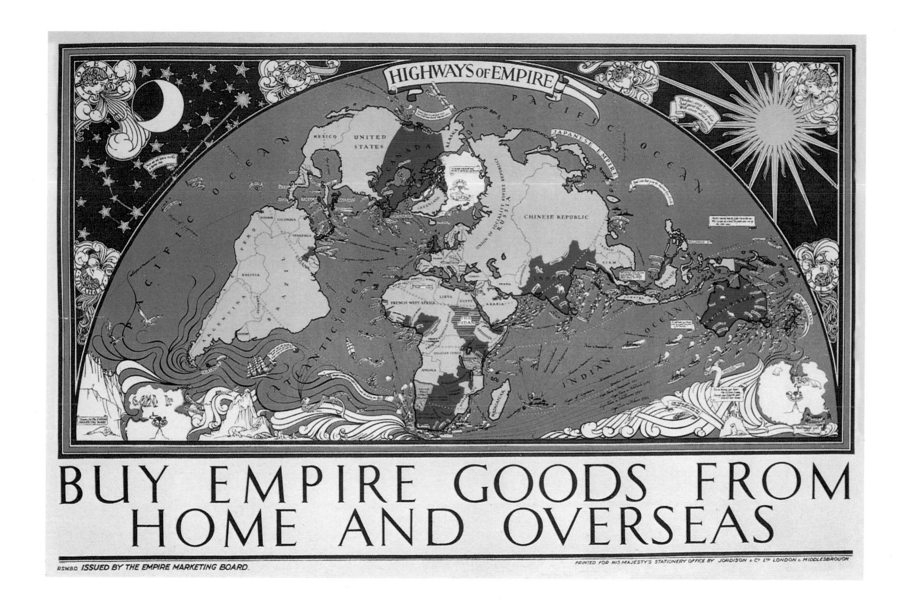

Year: 1927
Title: From home and overseas
Client: Empire Marketing Board
Artist: MacDonald Gill

The Empire Marketing Board existed for only eight years, but in that time it commissioned over 800 designs, many of which were made into posters displayed on commercial hoardings. This one, by MacDonald Gill, was the very first poster to be produced for the board and it was unveiled on New Year's Day 1927. (See also page 30)

Year: 1927
Title: First thing every morning
Client: Eno's Fruit Salt
Agency: W. S. Crawford
Art Director: Ashley Havinden

The striking, graphical image created by art director Ashley Havinden for Eno's Fruit Salt took its influence from the Bauhaus movement. The poster endows the brand with a strong look and feel, is eye-catching and – appropriately for a health product – conveys a zest for life

Year: circa 1927
Title: Player's Please
Client: John Player & Sons
Artist: Unknown

The copyline for this tobacco brand was originally 'They're Player's and they please'. However, the story goes that the cigarette company's advertising manager heard a customer asking for 'Player's please' in a shop. He returned to his office, wrote the two words down in his neat handwriting, and thereafter the slogan was used exactly as he had written it

MOTOR MANUFACTURING

Year: 1928
Title: Motor Manufacturing
Client: Empire Marketing Board
Artist: Clive Gardiner

Established in 1926 to promote the products of the Empire, the Empire Marketing Board commissioned some of the best artists of the day for its campaigns (see also page 27). 'Motor Manufacturing', with its distinctive Constructivist style, was one of a six-part poster series entitled 'Empire Building Makes Busy Factories'

Year and title: 1928 Oil and petrol; 1920 Pouring oil cans; 1923 The leading line
Client: Shell
Artists: Oil and petrol: Frederick Clifford Harrison; Pouring oil cans and The leading line: Unknown

Some of the most beautiful posters of the century were produced for Shell. Few of the early posters included what today would be termed branding and, to a certain extent, Shell was merely providing the frames for a series of fine artworks by artists such as Paul Nash and Graham Sutherland. Nevertheless they certainly stand the test of time

GUINNESS
IS GOOD FOR YOU

If he can say as you can
Guinness is good for you
How grand to be a Toucan
Just think what Toucan do

GUINNESS

FOR STRENGTH

Year and title: 1934 Guinness for strength; 1929 Guinness is good for you;
1935 How grand to be a Toucan
Client: Arthur Guinness Sons & Company
Agency: S.H. Benson
Art Director/Artist: John Gilroy
Copywriters: Guinness for strength: Unknown; Guinness is good for you: Robert Bevan;
How grand to be a toucan: Dorothy L. Sayers

This is possibly the most famous British advertising campaign of
all time. Certainly the posters put out by Guinness between 1929
and 1969 rank among the nation's favourites. Their success can
largely be attributed to the talents of John Gilroy who was art
director at the S.H. Benson advertising agency. His bold illustrative
style and cheeky sense of humour carried the campaign for 40
years. Novelist Dorothy L. Sayers wrote the tongue-twisting copy on
the Toucan execution

Year: circa 1935
Title: As the crow flies
Client: British Airways
Artist: Theyre Lee-Elliott

British Airways was a very
young company without an
established logo when
Theyre Lee-Elliott designed
this strong, graphical poster
for the airline. The slogan and
image combine to create a
sense of power and speed

Did you **MACLEAN** your teeth to-day Daisy ? *It's a cert, Gert.*

Year: 1938
Title: Daisy and Gert
Client: Beechams
Photographer: Unknown

This jaunty toothpaste campaign pioneered the use of celebrities – in this case the comedy duo of Elsie and Doris Waters – to endorse a product. It was also an early example of the use of photography rather than illustration in billboard advertising

Year: 1938
Title: Go out into the country
Client: London Transport
Artist: Graham Sutherland

Graham Sutherland designed this surreal image for London Transport which had a reputation for giving its commissioned artists an open brief. As a result, some of the best posters of the century were created on its behalf

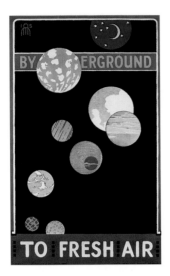

-KEEPS LONDON GOING

Year and title: 1939 Keeps London going;
1915 To fresh air; 1929 No wet, no cold
Client: London Transport
Artists: Keeps London going: Man Ray;
To Fresh air: Maxwell Armfield;
No wet, no cold: Manner

These are just three of many wonderful posters
produced for London Transport before the
Second World War. The main picture is by
avant-garde painter, filmmaker, philosopher,
Dadaist and surrealist Man Ray

"Of course there's no harm in your knowing!"

CARELESS TALK COSTS LIVES

Year: 1940
Title: Careless talk costs lives
Client: Ministry of Information
Artist: Cyril Kenneth Bird Fougasse

"Strictly between you + me...."

CARELESS TALK COSTS LIVES

"........ but for Heaven's sake don't say I told you!"

CARELESS TALK COSTS LIVES

Don't forget that walls have ears!

CARELESS TALK COSTS LIVES

Cartoonist Fougasse, who worked at *Punch* when he created these illustrations for the Ministry of Information, lent a refreshing sense of humour to the Second World War propaganda machine. The campaign caught the popular imagination and even prompted the then Princess Elizabeth to remark: 'How carelessly we should have talked during the war but for Fougasse'

Year: 1940
Title: Dig for victory
Client: War Office
Artist: Unknown

This is one of the most memorable images and copylines created during the Second World War to encourage people to do their bit. Almost crude in its simplicity, it drives its message home convincingly

'BACK ROOM BOYS'

BUS MAINTENANCE

'THEY ALSO SERVE'

'THEY ALSO SERVE'

'THEY ALSO SERVE'

Year: 1942
Titles: They also serve
Client: London Transport
Artist: Fred Taylor

These posters formed part of a series commissioned by London Transport. They were designed to boost morale during the darkest days of the Second World War and they highlighted the invaluable contribution of the workers at home who kept Britain going

Year: 1942
Title: Grow your own food
Client: Ministry of Information
Artist: Abram Games

Abram Games was the official poster designer of the Second World War and this poster clearly demonstrates his skill for combining visual elements with text to create an arresting and memorable image

Year: 1942
Title: Your talk may kill your comrades
Client: War Office
Artist: Abram Games

Of all his poster work, Abram Games rated
this is personal favourite. He created a
dramatic graphical composition that was
unusual in depicting allied men being killed.
But its message to the general public was
conveyed all the more powerfully for that

41

Year: 1945
Title: Think ahead write instead
Client: General Post Office
Artist: Hans Schleger (Zéró)

Graphic designer Hans Schleger, who signed himself Zéró, was one of many commercial artists commissioned by the British government to produce posters during the war. Here, in a beautifully composed image, the public is urged to write letters rather than use the telephone

Year: 1946
Title: Keep death off the road
Client: Ministry of Information
Artist: William Little

Like many of the campaigns produced by the government's public service information department, this one does not pull its punches. The haunting look on the face of the 'black widow' struck a chord with the public, many of whom found the poster distasteful when it first appeared in 1946

Year: 1948
Title: With gin this is it
Client: Martini UK
Agency: W.S. Crawford
Artist: Hans Schleger (Zéró)

Hans Schleger adeptly integrated words and image in this striking poster for the Martini vermouth brand where the bottle becomes the glass ... becomes the concept of a 'gin and Italian' drink

men who mean business read
THE FINANCIAL TIMES
every day

Year: 1951
Title: Men who mean business
Client: The *Financial Times*
Artist: Abram Games

This was the first in a series of eight posters by Abram Games designed to increase readership of the 'pink paper'. Using humour to promote a serious newspaper was a new approach at the time

The skilful fusing of image, concept and text in advertising reached its zenith in the 1950s with posters such as this one – before television became the predominant commercial medium and posters took second place. Tom Eckersley, who designed this ad for the Post Office, was a particularly adept poster artist (see also page 51)

Year: circa 1952
Title: Four pence minimum foreign rate
Client: General Post Office
Artist: Tom Eckersley

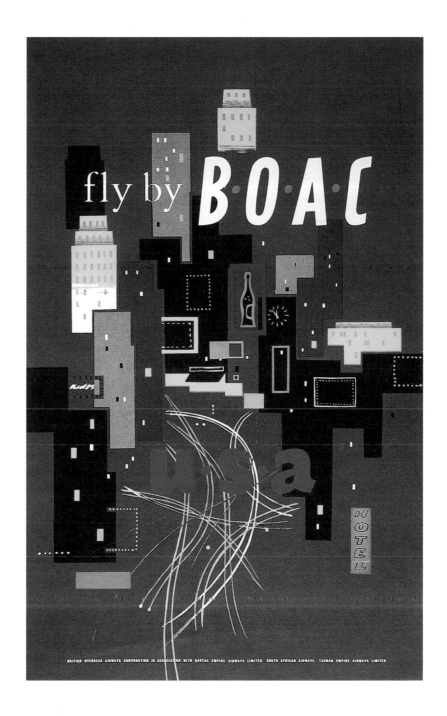

Year: 1954
Title: USA
Client: BOAC
Artists: Dick Negus, Philip Sharland

Neither an aircraft nor an airline logo are present here, only the angular excitement of New York in a view of Times Square which is representative of a particular graphical style popular in the 1950s. Dick Negus and Philip Sharland produced a series of posters for BOAC

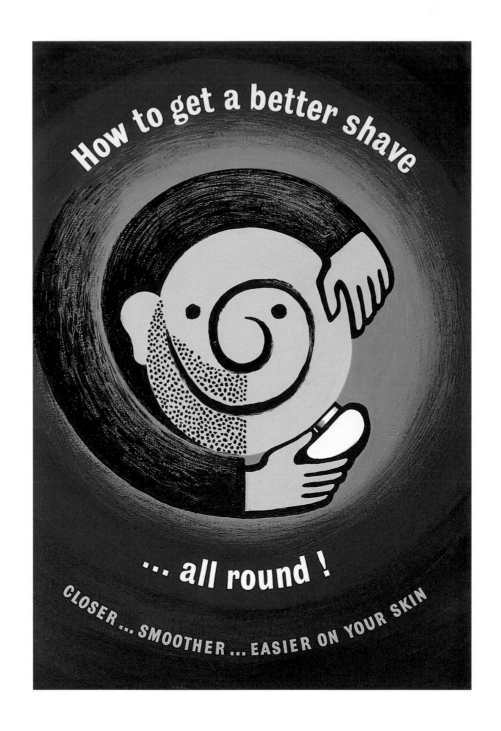

Year: 1955
Title: Better shave all round
Client: Philishave
Artist: F.H.K. Henrion

Taking his cue from the product – in
this case the Philishave razor's circular
head – poster artist F.H.K. Henrion
here cleverly integrated the message
into his design

Year: 1957
Title: Go to work on an egg
Client: British Egg Marketing Board
Agency: Mather & Crowther
Art Director: Ruth Gill
Copywriters: Fay Weldon, Mary Gowing
Photographer: Len Fulford

When novelist Fay Weldon worked at the Mather & Crowther advertising agency, she was instrumental in creating this, one of the all-time classic advertising slogans. Interestingly, the public did not take to its eggs being stamped with a lion hallmark – they didn't believe they were fresh – and the idea was abandoned

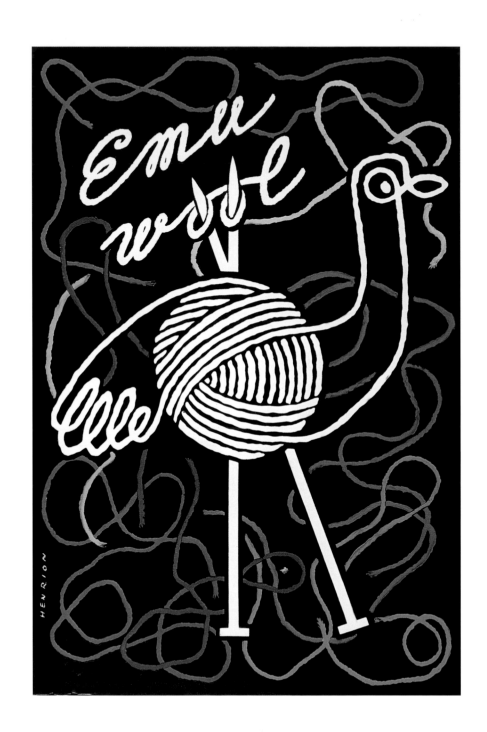

Year: 1958
Title: Emu Wool
Client: Emu Wool
Artist: F.H.K. Henrion

In this poster F.H.K Henrion cleverly 'knits' the brand name – not an obvious one for a type of wool – with the product so that, for the consumer, the two become inextricably linked

Good mornings begin with **Gillette**

Year: circa 1958
Title: Good mornings begin with Gillette
Client: Gillette Industries
Agency: W.S. Crawford
Artist: Tom Eckersley

Tom Eckersley created this popular campaign for Gillette in the late 1950s. The ads always featured two characters – one clean-shaven and one bearded. The visual elements worked better than the none-too-snappy copy which, in one magazine execution featuring two Santas, read: 'Tradition's important but tends to look weird, use a Blue Gillette blade with the sharpest edge ever and every tough whisker with ease it will sever'

Year: 1958
Title: Drinka Pinta Milka Day
Client: National Milk Publicity Council
Agency: Mather & Crowther
Copywriter: Bertrand Whitehead

The story goes that it was in fact the client – the Executive Officer of the National Milk Publicity Council – who came up with this famous copyline to promote his wares. The advertising agency's creative department was none too impressed but their boss, the late, great David Ogilvy, overruled them and the ad ran to wide acclaim

Year: 1959
Title: Unzipp a banana
Client: Elders & Fyffes
Agency: Mather & Crowther

Advertising slogans became very popular in the 1950s and this one, on behalf of Britain's three main banana importers, was an instant hit. The sexual suggestiveness of the idea broke new barriers but it captured the public's imagination

STOP NUCLEAR SUICIDE CAMPAIGN FOR NUCLEAR DISARMAMENT 2 CARTHUSIAN ST LONDON EC1

Year: 1963
Title: Stop nuclear suicide
Client: Campaign for Nuclear Disarmament
Artist: F.H.K. Henrion

F.H.K. Henrion's simple but striking image of a skull superimposed on the mushroom cloud of a nuclear explosion made for an arresting poster for CND in 1963. It was a poster designed for the time – a period of intensive political activism for civil rights and against nuclear weapons and the war in Vietnam

Year: 1966
Title: Battle of Hastings
Client: Guinness UK
Agency: S.H. Benson
Artist: Stanley Penn

Guinness advertisements have a special place in advertising history (see pages 32 and 62). This amusing poster – which comments on two different types of conquest – is a testament to the advantages of being opportunistic

Year: 1967
Title: Beanz meanz Heinz
Client: H.J. Heinz
Agency: Young & Rubicam
Art Director: Jean Bird
Copywriter: Mo Drake
Photographer: Tony Copeland

Advertising lore has it that this line was written – by
one Maurice Drake from the Young & Rubicam
agency – over two pints of bitter in the local pub.
The slogan certainly set the education fraternity on
edge with its deliberate misspellings

Year: 1967
Title: For God's sake
Client: Salvation Army
Agency: KMP Partnership
Photographer: Peter Atherton

The original line for this striking campaign was 'For God Sake, Give us a Pound'. It was softened by the inclusion of the word 'Care' at the client's request, but lost none of its power, or poignancy, as a result

Would you be more careful if it was you that got pregnant?

Anyone married or single can get advice on contraception from the **Family Planning Association.**
Margaret Pyke House, 27-35 Mortimer Street, London W1 N 8BQ. Tel. 01-636 9135.

The Health Education Council

Year: 1969
Title: Pregnant Man
Client: Health Education Council
Agency: Cramer Saatchi
Art Director: Bill Atherton
Copywriter: Jeremy Sinclair
Photographer: Alan Brooking

This poster is now regarded as a classic although at the time many thought it overstepped the boundaries of good taste. Conceived by the agency that went on to become Saatchi & Saatchi, the elegant simplicity of the creative idea shines through

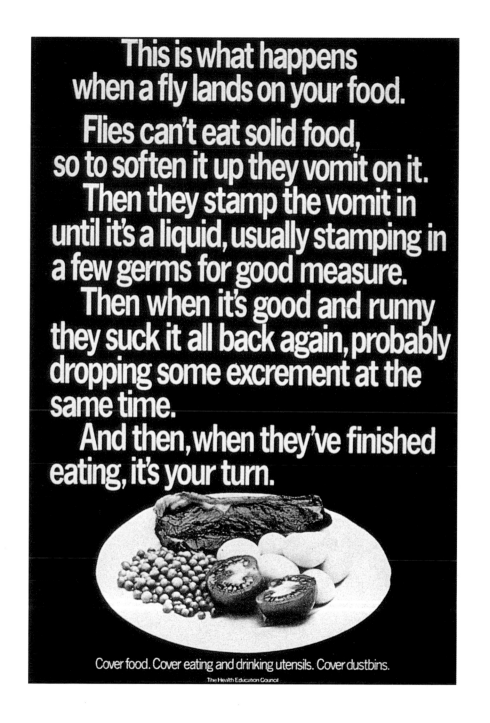

This is what happens when a fly lands on your food.

Flies can't eat solid food, so to soften it up they vomit on it. Then they stamp the vomit in until it's a liquid, usually stamping in a few germs for good measure. Then when it's good and runny they suck it all back again, probably dropping some excrement at the same time. And then, when they've finished eating, it's your turn.

Cover food. Cover eating and drinking utensils. Cover dustbins.

The Health Education Council

Year: 1970
Title: Fly
Client: Health Education Council
Agency: Cramer Saatchi
Art Director: John Hegarty
Copywriters: Charles Saatchi, Michael Coughlan

The story goes that the copy for this stomach-turning poster originally appeared in a government pamphlet. The agency takes the credit for deciding to leave well alone – as well as for adding the final line

Year: 1971
Title: Accountancy was my life
until I discovered Smirnoff
Client: Smirnoff
Agency: Young & Rubicam
Art Director: David Tree
Copywriter: John Bacon
Photography: Hans Fuhrer

The idea that Smirnoff has the
power to transform is still used
today in the vodka brand's
advertising. In this campaign, for
which there were several
memorable executions, the quirky
humour is all in the writing

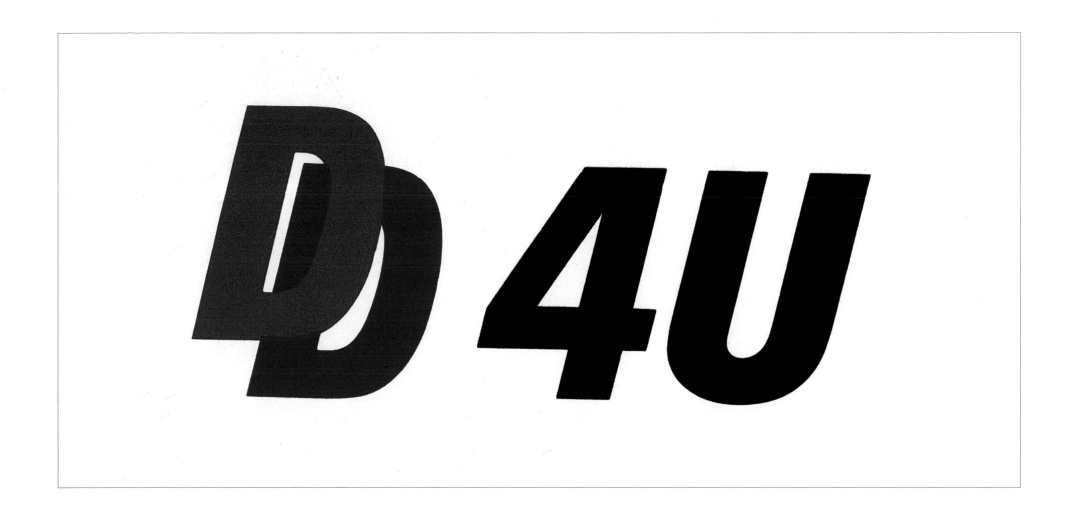

Year: 1972
Title: DD4U
Client: Double Diamond
Agency: The Kirkwood Company
Art Director: Paul Eastwood
Copywriter: Martin Hodges

This clever poster for Double Diamond beer
demonstrated the art of the simple and
gave passers-by pause for thought

"I've never tried it because I don't like it."

Year: 1974
Title: I've never tried it because I don't like it
Client: Arthur Guinness & Sons
Agency: J. Walter Thompson
Art Director: David Barker
Copywriters: Jeremy Bullmore, Tom Rayfield

Apparently the idea for this poster emerged from a research group organised by the agency, J. Walter Thompson. One of the members of the group being questioned about Guinness said something to this effect and a great advertising copyline was born. It was another good idea in a long tradition of memorable Guinness advertisements (see pages 32 and 55)

When was the last time a man said you had a great pair of jeans?

Pretty Polly brings back lovely legs.

PP
PRETTY POLLY

Year: 1976
Title: Great pair of jeans
Client: Pretty Polly
Agency: Collett Dickenson Pearce & Partners
Art Director: Ted Ekman
Copywriter: Joanne Mond
Photograph: Barry Lategan

Very much of its time, this cheeky
campaign for Pretty Polly turned heads
and – reportedly – caused more than a
few road accidents

Year: 1976
Title: Porky and Best
Agency: Collett Dickenson Pearce
Creative Director: John Salmon
Art Director: Alan Waldie
Copywriter: Terry Lovelock
Photographer: David Thorpe

The advertising team that created this
engaging poster reportedly had a lot of
fun coming up with ideas to promote
the famous British banger

MIDDLE TAR As defined by H.M. Government
H.M. Government Health Departments' WARNING: CIGARETTES CAN SERIOUSLY DAMAGE YOUR HEALTH

Year and title: 1977 Pyramids; 1977 Mousehole; 1978 Bird cage
Client: Gallaher/Benson & Hedges
Agency: Collett Dickenson Pearce
Art Director: Neil Godfrey
Copywriter: Tony Brignull
Photographer: Jimmy Wormser

In pioneering the use of surreal imagery, this famous Benson & Hedges campaign marked a turning point in tobacco advertising and was widely imitated thereafter. Forbidden to say anything about the product, the agency chose to do away with copy altogether and created a new kind of art form

Year: 1978
Title: Labour isn't working
Client: Conservative Party
Agency: Saatchi & Saatchi
Art Director: Martyn Walsh
Copywriter: Andrew Rutherford

With this poster the Saatchi brothers changed the rules of elections by introducing aggressive advertising techniques into party political campaigning. The poster is often cited as having been instrumental in the fall of James Callaghan's Labour administration and the coming to power of Margaret Thatcher. Its stark depiction of an unemployment office queue and the copyline – with its clever double meaning – was aimed at traditional Labour supporters who feared for their jobs

Year: 1978
Title: No head
Client: Barker & Dobson
Agency: Boase Massimi Pollitt
Copywriter: Dave Trott
Art Director: Derrick Hass
Illustrator: Larry Learmonth

The advertiser here assumes a certain
knowledge among consumers – namely
that Victory V lozenges are so strong
they are liable to 'blow your head off'.
The Magritte-style image is both funny
and memorable

The new Fiat 132.

Year: 1979
Title: Wolf in sheep's clothing
Client: Fiat
Agency: Collett Dickenson Pearce
Art Director: Neil Godfrey
Copywriter: Tony Brignull
Photographer: Alan Brooking

This poster for Fiat was designed to convey the power that lay under the bonnet of the new 132 model. It ran for two weeks before billboards showing the car were unveiled

SCOTCH AND GINGER.

Year: 1979
Title: Scotch and Ginger
Client: White Horse Distillers
Agency: French Cruttenden Osborn
Art Director: Graham Norways
Copywriter: Nick Hazzard
Photographer: Lester Bookbinder

A literal interpretation made for a humourous visual
pun in this campaign by FCO for White Horse whisky

ROOSTER
BOOSTER

PAXO

Year: 1980
Title: Rooster booster
Client: RHM Foods
Agency: Collett Dickenson Pearce
Art Director: Peter Ibbitson
Copywriter: Peter Ibbitson
Photographer: Billy Wrencher
Typographer: Nigel Dawson

The copywriter's art is shown to its best
effect in this poster that places the product
at the centre of a simple but powerful idea

Year: 1980
Titles: H2 Eau, Picasseau
Client: Aqualac-Perrier
Agency: Leo Burnett
Creative Director: Bob Stanners
Art Directors: Mike Trumble, Dougie Buntrock
Copywriter: Colin Campbell
Typographer: Cliff Butler
Photographer: John Turner

This series of posters was founded on puns – both literal and visual. The campaign proved so popular that it ran for over a decade

You're in this cell
for your
own protection.

Polo. VW

Year: 1980
Title: Cell
Client: Volkswagen
Agency: Doyle Dane Bernbach
Creative Director: Dawson Yeoman
Art Director: Peter Harold
Copywriter: Barbara Nokes
Typographer: Peter Harold
Photographer: Geoff Senior

Volkswagen is associated with great advertising. The campaigns created by agency Doyle Dane Bernbach in the United States for models such as the VW Beetle are hailed as among the most inventive of the century. There have been a few gems in the UK too, notably this poster for the VW Polo

Heineken refreshes the parts other beers cannot reach.

Year. 1980
Title: Halo
Client: Whitbread
Agency: Collett Dickenson Pearce
Creative Director: John Kelley
Art Director: Tony Kaye
Copywriter: Paul Weinberger
Photographer/Illustrator: Reid Miles

The 'Heineken refreshes...' campaign ran for many years. This poster, depicting how the beer could transform the completely immoral J.R. Ewing from TV soap opera Dallas, showed the campaign at its best

This much lead in this much pencil.

Parker Continuous Feed Pencils.

◇ PARKER

Year: 1981
Title: This much lead in this much pencil
Client: Parker Pen Company
Agency: Collett Dickenson Pearce
Creative Director: John Salmon
Art Director: John Horton
Copywriter: Richard Foster
Typographer: Maggie Lewis
Photographer: Graham Ford

A clear demonstration of one of the product's selling points – probably taken directly from the client's brief – is interpreted with rude humour in this Parker Pen advertisement

Year: 1982
Title: It also sticks handles to teapots
Client: Ciba Geigy
Agency: Foote Cone & Belding
Art Director: Robert Kitchen
Copywriter: Ian Potter

Arguably the most audacious use of a billboard ever, this clever campaign clearly demonstrates that the product, Araldite glue, does what it says on the packaging. The campaign set a precedent in using the poster as a three-dimensional medium. The great and the good of the advertising world regularly vote it as one of the 'best of the best'

Year: 1982
Title: Black sheep
Client: Levi Strauss
Agency: Bartle Bogle Hegarty
Creative Director: John Hegarty
Art Director: John Hegarty
Copywriter: Barbara Nokes

According to John Hegarty, who art directed this poster promoting black denim, Levi Strauss was unsure about running an advertisement that did not show its jeans. In the end, however, the idea's quirkiness won the company over

Pancake day. February 15th.

Year: 1983
Title: Pancake day
Client: Colmans of Norwich
Agency: Foote Cone & Belding
Creative Director: Andrew Cracknell
Art Director: Gerard Stamp
Copywriter: Loz Simpson

It may take a second or two for passers-by to understand the picture – and the joke – but in that time they have been persuaded that pancake day is 'Jif lemon day'

McENROE SWEARS BY THEM.

NIKE

Year: 1983
Title: McEnroe swears by them
Client: Nike
Agency: FCO Univas
Art Director: Ian Potter
Copywriter: Chris Herring

Since its launch, Nike has built its brand and its reputation on the back of consistently excellent advertising (see page 97). Posters don't get much more effective than this one which merely juxtaposes a straightforward photograph of the product with a cracking one-liner. The poster cleverly refers to tennis star John McEnroe's propensity to hurl abuse at those refereeing his matches

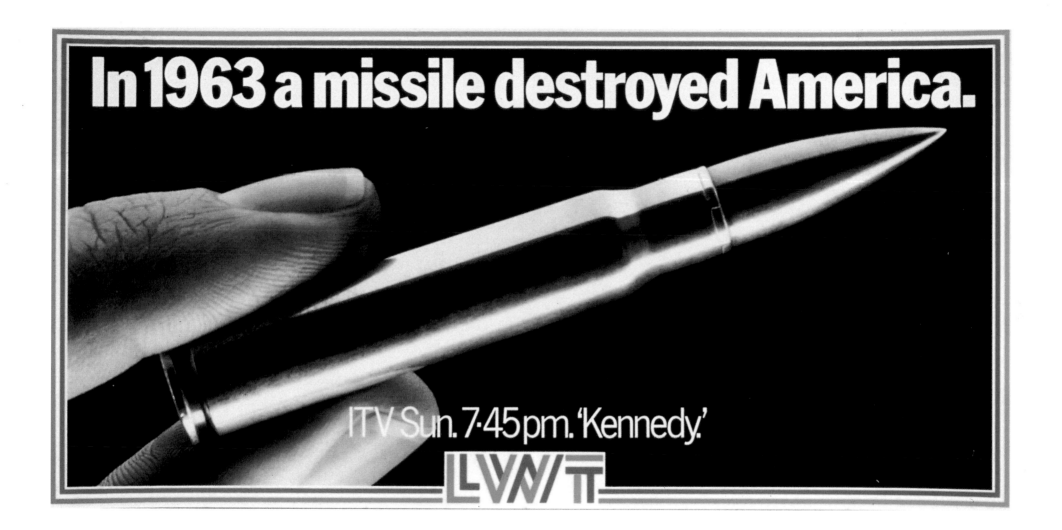

Year: 1984
Title: Missile
Client: London Weekend Television
Agency: Gold Greenlees Trott
Art Director: Sam Hurford
Copywriter: Paul Grubb
Typographer: Ros Walters
Photographer: Ian Giles

If the art of the poster boils down to a simple visual
supported by a clever headline that intrigues the viewer,
then this must stand as a model campaign

Year: 1984
Title: Map of Australia
Client: Watney Mann Truman
Agency: Hedger Mitchell Stark
Art Director: Warren Brown
Copywriter: Jeff Stark
Photographer: John Turner
Illustrator: David Draper

This memorable ad helped put Foster's on the map. Associating the brand with its country of origin has been at the heart of the brewer's advertising over the years

CHURCHILL

IMAGINE WHAT
LONDON WILL BE LIKE RUN
BY WHITEHALL.

SAY NO TO NO SAY.

Year: 1985
Title: Red tape
Client: Greater London Council
Agency: Boase Massimi Pollitt
Art Director: Peter Gatley
Copywriter: John Pallant
Typographer: Gary Whipps

The Greater London Council under Ken Livingstone became
such a thorn in Margaret Thatcher's side when she was
prime minister that she decided the only solution was to
abolish it. This poster, created by Boase Massimi Pollitt to
defend the GLC, used the medium in a highly original way
and it was much admired. It did not, however, succeed in
saving the GLC from abolition

Photo: David Bailey

It takes up to 40 dumb animals to make a fur coat.

But only one to wear it.

GREENPEACE

If you don't want animals to be gassed, electrocuted, trapped or strangled, don't buy a fur coat. 36 Graham Street London N1 8LL. Tel: 01-251 3020

Year: 1986
Title: Dumb animals
Client: Greenpeace
Agency: Yellowhammer
Creative Director: Jeremy Pemberton
Art Director: Jeremy Pemberton
Copywriter: Alan Page
Typographer: Jeremy Pemberton
Photographer: David Bailey

Sometimes shock tactics are called for. In this case, a dramatic photograph by David Bailey, combined with a superbly pointed copyline, combined to drive the message home

Year: 1987
Title: It is are you?
Client: The *Independent*
Agency: Saatchi & Saatchi
Deputy Creative Director: Tim Mellors
Art Director: Digby Atkinson
Copywriters: Peter Russell, Tim Mellors
Typographer: Digby Atkinson

When this campaign broke, the *Independent* claimed it had what in advertising terms is known as a 'unique selling proposition' – namely that it was the only independently owned – and therefore independent thinking – English broadsheet newspaper.

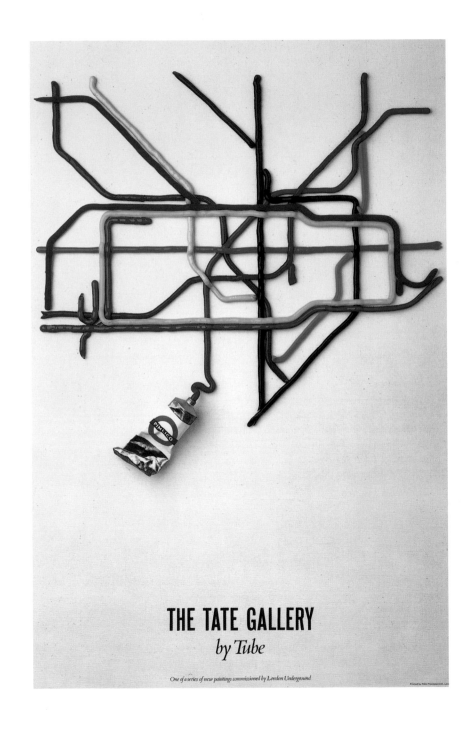

Year: 1987
Title: Tate Gallery
Client: London Transport
Agency: The Fine White Line
Creative Director: David Hughes
Designer: David Booth
Modelmakers: Malcolm Fowler, Nancy Fowler

London Transport's advertising agencies have a lot to live up to, given the magnificent posters that were created for the tube network before the Second World War (see pages 35, 36 and 39). This highly original idea met the challenge and has become a contemporary classic

OR BUY A VOLVO.

Year: 1987
Title: Cotton wool
Client: Volvo
Agency: Abbott Mead Vickers
Art Director: Ron Brown
Copywriter: David Abbott
Photographer: Bob Miller

Volvo has consistently used the issue of safety in its brand advertising (see also page 87). This poster aimed to demonstrate – with a light touch – the company's commitment to protecting passengers in its cars

Year: 1988
Title: Mechanic
Client: Unilever
Agency: J. Walter Thompson
Creative Director: Allen Thomas
Art Director: Annie Carlton
Copywriter: Sandra Leamon
Photographer: David Fairman

With their use of bold, flat colour, the beautiful posters in this campaign paid homage to advertisements for Persil from the early 1900s. They made a refreshing change from the somewhat crude ads often used to promote soap powders

Year: 1988
Title: Cages save lives
Client: Volvo
Agency: Abbott Mead Vickers
Creative Director: David Abbott
Art Director: Mark Roalfe
Copywriter: Robert Campbell
Typographer: Jo Hoza

Tenaciously sticking with its message concerning the safety of its cars (see also page 85), Volvo's advertising agency found a superbly powerful image for this poster in 1988

"I never read The Economist."

Management trainee. Aged 42.

How to win at board games.

The Economist

The Economist

Year and title: 1989 Management trainee; 1991 Keyhole;
1993 Board games
Client: *The Economist*
Agency: Abbott Mead Vickers SMS
Creative Director: David Abbott
Art Directors: Ron Brown, John Horton
Copywriters: David Abbott, Richard Foster
Typographer: Jo Hoza

Many of the best posters work because they act on the premise that 'less is more'. In this acclaimed campaign for *The Economist* – which is as popular today as it was when it was launched over a decade ago – the skills of the copywriter, David Abbott, come to the fore. The deceptive simplicity of the posters belies their strong branding and the campaign has developed an enduring relationship with the consumer

Year: 1990
Title: Cash, Czech or American Express
Client: Queen's Club Tennis Tournament
Agency: Lowe Howard-Spink
Art Director: Simon Butler
Copywriter: Gethin Stout
Illustrator: Sebastian Kruger
Typographer: Brian Hill

It's not often that the subject matter of an ad
lends itself to a such superlative verbal pun as
on this poster for the Queen's Club tennis
tournament. The ad features Australian Pat
Cash, Czech Ivan Lendl and American
John McEnroe

AUSTRALIANS WOULDN'T GIVE A XXXX FOR ANYTHING ELSE.

Year: 1991
Title: Crocodile
Client: Allied Breweries
Agency: Saatchi & Saatchi
Creative Director: James Lowther
Art Director: Zelda Malan
Copywriter: Peter Barry
Typographer: Roger Kennedy
Photographer: Peter Lavery
Retouching: Dan Tierney

The 'laddish' humour used in this campaign for
Castlemaine struck just the right note with the
target market, while the copyline quickly
entered the collective vocabulary

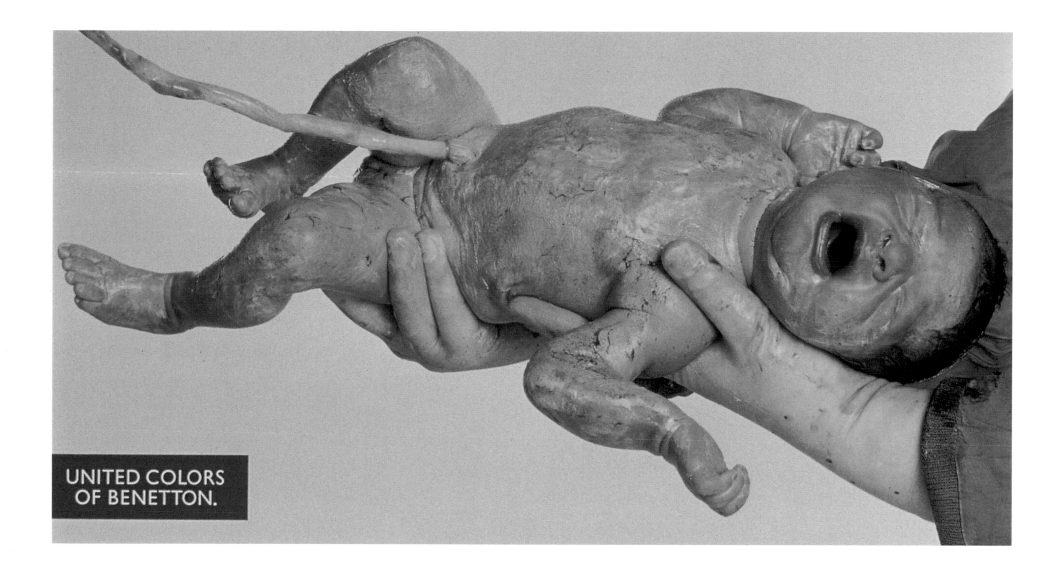

UNITED COLORS
OF BENETTON.

Year: 1991
Title: Newborn baby
Client: Benetton
Creative Director: Oliviero Toscani
Photographer: Oliviero Toscani

Love it or loathe it, you cannot ignore this controversial campaign. The images Oliviero Toscani chose for his Benetton ads certainly met his objective of 'making people think'. This particular poster was banned in the US and the UK, and many people felt others – including one showing a man dying of Aids and another in which a black woman nurses a white baby – overstepped the mark

Year: 1991
Title: Ketchup
Client: H.J. Heinz
Agency: BSB Dorland
Creative Director: Andrew Cracknell
Art Director: Gerard Stamp
Copywriter: Loz Simpson
Illustrator: Robin Heighway-Bury

This umbrella campaign for Heinz products used
the poster medium to good effect. The large-scale,
beautifully drafted illustrations conveyed positive
associations about the brand

Year: 1991
Title: Hens
Client: Holsten Distributors
Agency: GGT
Creative Director: Tim Mellors
Art Director: Graham Fink
Copywriter: Tim Mellors
Typographer: Len Cheeseman
Illustrator: David Juniper
Retouching: Tapestry

Ironically for an advertisement, this poster was almost a lesson in 'un-branding'. Those in the know knew, by virtue of the typeface and colours alone, which brand was being promoted. Others had to spend a second or two working it out. Either way the public was drawn into the poster

"I want to be in the other poster."

PRUDENTIAL
SAVINGS PLANS
0800 444 100

Holiday 92°

The holiday of a lifetime. Every time.   SUNFINDER HOLIDAYS.

"I want to save for a rainy day."

PRUDENTIAL
SAVINGS PLANS

Year: 1992
Title: Other poster
Client: Prudential
Agency: WCRS
Creative Director: Alan Tilby
Art Director: Andy Dibb
Copywriter: Gary Knight
Typographer: Kim Le Liboux

Marshall McLuhan said 'the medium is the message' which is ably demonstrated in this twin-poster execution for Prudential

LOW TAR As defined by H.M. Government DANGER: Government Health WARNING: **CIGARETTES CAN SERIOUSLY DAMAGE YOUR HEALTH**

Year and title: 1993 Slash; 1993 Can Can; 1996 Cheesegrater
Client: Gallaher Tobacco
Creative Directors: Paul Arden, James Lowther, Simon Dicketts
Art Directors: Paul Arden, Carlos Bogue, Louis Bogue
Copywriters: Charles Saatchi, Keith Bickel, Pete Cain
Photographers: Graham Ford, François Gillet, Douglas Brothers

Restrictions on cigarette advertising led to a new, surreal approach to the genre, as shown with these posters for Silk Cut cigarettes (see also page 65). The core concept of a cut in a piece of silk was developed into a series of clever executions

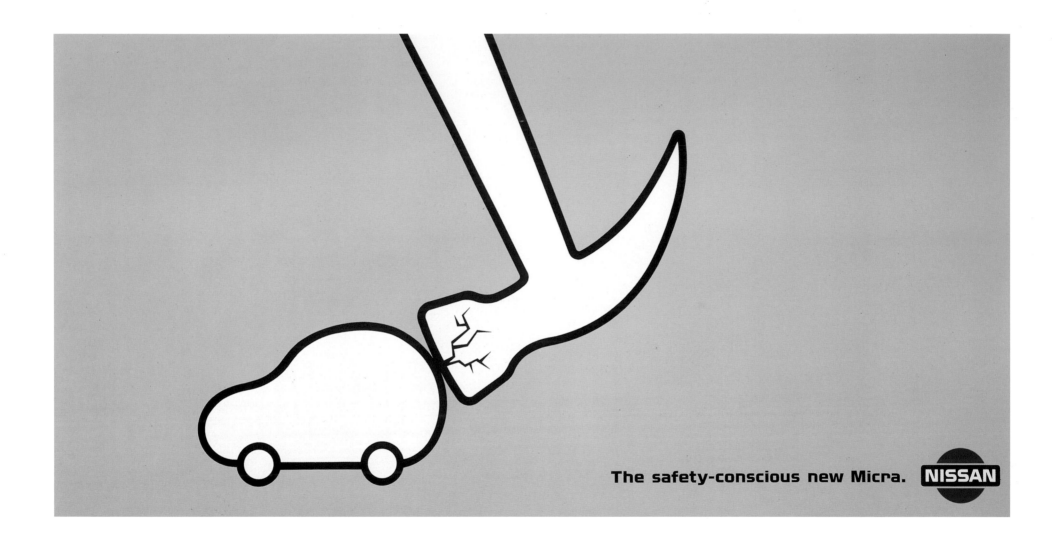

The safety-conscious new Micra. **NISSAN**

Year: 1993
Title: Hammer
Client: Nissan
Agency: TBWA HKR
Creative Director: Trevor Beattie
Art Director: Steve Chatham
Copywriter: Trevor Beattie
Typographer: Tivy Davies
Illustrator: Steve Chatham

Few car makers would approve advertising that turned their new model into a cartoon. This launch campaign for the Nissan Micra therefore testified to a very brave client. The simple line drawings gave the car a friendly personality and the posters stood out among the plethora of predictable car advertising

96

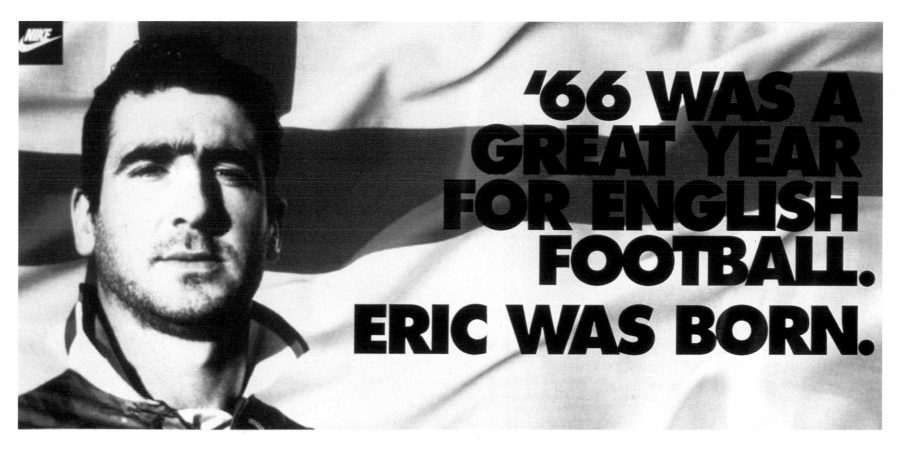

Year: 1994
Titles: '66 was a great year; Sampras to serve; Behind every great goalkeeper
Client: Nike
Agency: Simons Palmer Denton Clemmow & Johnson
Creative directors: Chris Palmer, Mark Denton
Art Directors: Andy McKay, Tiger Savage, Gary Martin
Copywriters: Giles Montgomery, Paul Silburn, Mark Goodwin
Typographer: John Tisdall
Photographers: Tim O'Sullivan, Seamus Ryan, Malcolm Venville

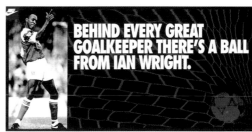

Between them, the agencies that have worked for Nike, such as Chiat/Day and Wieden & Kennedy in the US and Simons Palmer Denton Clemmow & Johnson in the UK, have produced some of the most outstanding advertising of the past three decades. The sportswear company has always put marketing at the centre of its business strategy. It has also taken celebrity endorsement to a new level, as these three executions show

Year: 1994
Title: Red high heels
Client: Pirelli
Agency: Young & Rubicam
Creative Director: Mike Cozens
Art Director: Graham Norways
Copywriter: Ewan Patterson
Photographer: Annie Liebowitz

This poster was persuasive because it successfully juxtaposed an arresting image (that of Olympic gold medallist Carl Lewis wearing a woman's high-heel shoes) with a headline – the former unarguably underlining the truth of the latter. The idea was also completely relevant to tyres

THE ONE AND ONLY

Wonderbra®

THE ORIGINAL PUSH-UP PLUNGE BRA. AVAILABLE IN SIZES 32-38 ABC.

Year: 1994
Title: Hello boys
Client: Playtex
Agency: TBWA HKR
Creative Director: Trevor Beattie
Art Director: Nigel Rose
Copywriter: Nigel Rose
Typographer: Tivy Davies
Photographer: Ellen Von Unwerth

This is the poster that prompted a thousand column inches.
Although over 20 posters ran in the Wonderbra campaign, this is the
one that captured the imagination of both the public and the media.
Everyone from the *Financial Times* to the *Sun* discussed the merits –
or otherwise – of the 'Hello Boys' ad

Year: 1995
Title: Beaver España
Client: Club 18-30
Agency: Saatchi and Saatchi
Creative Director: Simon Dicketts
Art Director: David Hillyard
Copywriter: Ed Robinson
Typographer: Lynn Mackintosh

This controversial campaign had the effect of
polarising consumer opinion. While it
appalled those who needed to have its
message translated (ie, anyone over 30), it
thrilled the people it was aimed at

Year: 1996
Title: Tall legs
Client: Pretty Polly
Agency: TBWA
Creative Director: Trevor Beattie
Art Director: Steve Chatham
Copywriter: Trevor Beattie
Typographer: Tivy Davies
Photographer: Platon

This campaign took a whole new approach to billboards by turning them 180 degrees. In the advertising world the innovation was dubbed VMS, the 'vertical media strategy'. Some of the posters fell victim to Britain's 'hurricane' season, however, and were literally bent at the knees by October gales

101

fcuk fashion

Year: 1997
Title: Fcuk fashion
Client: French Connection
Agency: GGT
Art Director: Jay Pond-Jones
Copywriter: Trevor Beattie
Photographer: Neil Davenport
Typographer: Mick Tonello

Middle England was mortified when this poster campaign hit the
streets in 1997. French Connection was happy, however, as it
enjoyed a healthy rise in sales after the ads appeared

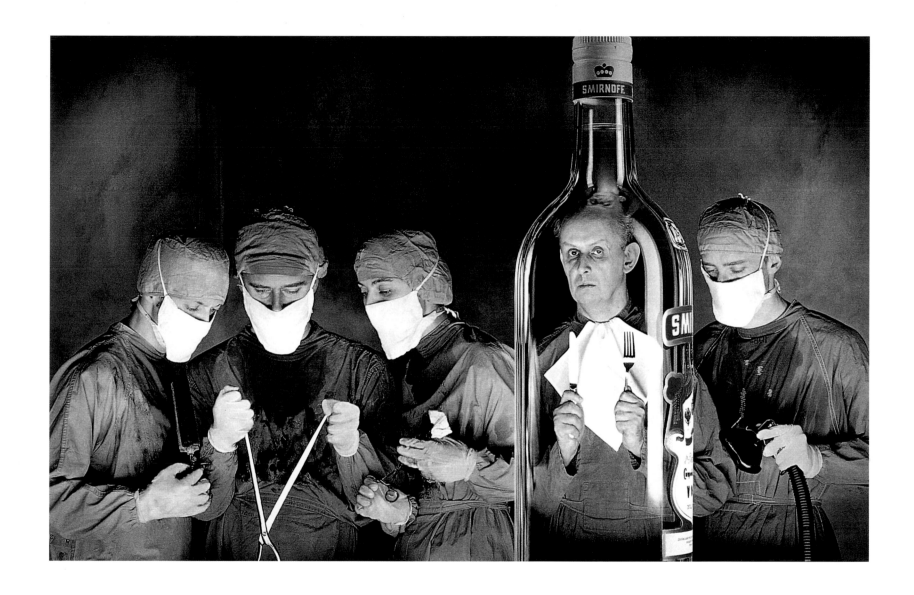

Year: 1997
Title: Surgeons
Client: Smirnoff
Agency: Lowe Howard-Spink
Art Director: Charles Inge
Copywriter: Charles Inge
Photographer: Andy Green

The viewer might flinch, but he or she is instantly involved
in this powerful image for Smirnoff. The poster conveys the
idea, constant to the vodka brand's advertising, that to
drink it changes one's perceptions

ABSOLUT PERFECTION.

Year: 1998
Title: Absolut Perfection
Client: The Absolut Company
Agency: TBWA
Creative Director: Carol Ann Fine
Art Director: Geoff Hayes
Photographer: Steve Bronstein

Absolut Vodka has proved to be one of the most innovative advertisers of the late 20th century. Its long-running campaign integrates the distinctive shape of the brand's bottle into a number of different contexts. The 'Perfection' idea was born in the early 1980s but first appeared as a poster in the UK in 1998

Year: 1998
Title: Beautiful daughter
Client: Irn-Bru
Agency: The Leith Agency
Creative Director: Gerry Farrell
Art Director: Alex Paton
Copywriter: Don Smith
Photographer: Euan Myles

A strangely named fizzy drink made its mark
with this irreverent, funny poster campaign
devised by The Leith Agency

Fly Virgin to the Caribbean from September.

virgin atlantic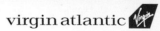

Year: 1998
Title: Caribbean
Client: Virgin Atlantic
Agency: Rainey Kelly Campbell Roalfe
Creative Directors: Mark Roalfe, Robert Campbell
Art Director: Martha Riley
Typographers: John Tisdall, Ryan Shellard

This bold advertisement for Richard Branson's airline worked
on two levels: it cleverly summed up the spirit of the
destination as well as the feel of the brand

Year: 1998
Title: Swear box
Client: Volkswagen
Agency: BMP DDB
Art Director: Paul Angus
Copywriter: Ted Heath
Typographer: Richard Bateman

This poster formed part of a wonderfully understated, price-led campaign that turned conventional car advertising on its head. It also obeyed all the rules of great poster advertising in being simple, effective and startling

PlayStation is a registered trademark of Sony Computer Entertainment Inc.

Year: 1999
Title: Nipples
Client: Sony Playstation
Agency: TBWA
Creative Director: Trevor Beattie
Art Director: Nick Hine
Copywriter: Paula Jackson
Photographer: Tomas Schelp

Only those truly initiated in the computer game world
understood this poster for Sony Playstation
immediately. For others it would taunt and tease. Either
way, it left an impression